THE DEADWORD DICTIONARY

A BOOK OF OUTDATED WORDS

Sasha Newborn, editor

MUDBORN PRESS   2014   SΔNTΔ BΔRBΔRΔ

MUDBORN PRESS

NOVELS AND SHORT STORIES

The First Detective, Poe   Hadji Murad, Tolstoy   Goblin Market, Rossetti
Frankenstein & Matilda, Mary Shelley   Surfing, Jack London   Ski, Doyle
Martian Testament, The Basement, Eight2Two   Benigna Machiavelli, Gilman

INKLINGS & BILINGUAL

Sobre Esta Praia (Sena)   Aztec Birth (Portugés)   At the Fallow's Edge (Ivask)
Italian for Opera Lovers   French for Food Lovers   Yiddish, You Say? Nu?
Mitos y Leyendas/Myths and Legends of Mexico   Berlin: Divided City

SPIRIT

Ghazals of Ghalib   Everlasting Gospel   Beechers Thru the 19th Century
The Gospel According to Tolstoy   Gandhi on the Bhagavad Gita

POETRY

Dante & His Circle.   Vita Nuova, Dante   Ovid, The Changes
Aurora Leigh, E.B. Browning   Sappho: Poems   Cretan Cycle, Coffey

BANDANNA BOOKS

STAGING SHAKESPEARE

shakespeareplaybook.com DIRECTOR'S PLAYBOOK SERIES

Hamlet   Merchant of Venice   Twelfth Night   Taming of the Shrew
A Midsummer Night's Dream Romeo and Juliet As You Like It Richard III
Henry V   Much Ado About Nothing   Macbeth   Othello
  plus   7 Plays with Transgender Characters   Falstaff: 4 Plays   Venus and Adonis

TEACHERS SECTION

Don't Panic: Procrastinator's Guide to Term Paper   First Person Intense
SUPPLEMENT EDITIONS
Areopagitica, John Milton   Apology of Socrates, Plato   Sappho, The Poems
  Leaves of Grass, Walt Whitman   Uncle Tom's Cabin, Harriet Beecher Stowe
Pi to 500k Decimal Places, Miller   Idea of a President, Madison

FOREWORD

The Deadword Dictionary was first written more than twenty years ago. I'm making some changes, based on further refinement of the concept, and also including an "Iffy" section. Here are the rules for the selection of Deadwords:

> Orphans, words used in only a single common
> expression, with no flexibility, such as "yore" as
> in "days of yore."

> Faux amis, words borrowed from another language _there is it is_
> but misunderstood or misapplied (à la mode)

> Obsolete words or phrases

> Iffy words—you decide whether they still have weight
> in today's language.

You might call this the rearview mirror perspective, with a "huh" under one's breath. Yeah? They really said that?

The English language is like a kitchen sponge: it picks up all the tiny pieces of we-don't-know-what but we need a word, so we'll just use this stray one from we-don't-care-where. But when did you last see a "doublet" or "spitoon" or use "whilom"—why keep them around? A little housecleaning is in order here.

Got your favorite overworked obsolete nugget? Send it in.

Sasha Newborn
January 2014

Some words, such as pregnant, retain a modern meaning, while an antique usage has disappeared (or should).

A

aback (taken aback): surprised

abaft: behind, to the rear, to the stern of a ship

abide : tolerate; dwell

abject (abject poverty): deep

abscond: (abscond with the funds): run off, escape

accidence : inflections, word order, accents

ace : very small amount, least

adamant : hard *(one)* substance; diamond

afeard : afraid

afield (far afield): away, off the subject, off the beaten path

affied : betrothed *affianced*

afoot (the game's afoot, Watson): begun, in action

aforethought (with malice aforethought): previously
     imagined

agog: astonished

agone : ago

alack: I regret

alackaday: I regret

alarum : fuss, ado, clamor

alas: too bad, I regret

albeit: though, although, even though

allayments : antidotes

alms-guest : person in temporary shelter

amerce: fine, punish

amidst: amid, in the middle of

amiss : out of proper order

amok (run amok): wild, crazy, berserk amongst: among

amuck (run amuck): wild

anent : concerning

anon: soon, immediately, right away

an't: if it

aplomb (with aplomb): coolheadedness, sangfroid,
    diplomacy

aright (if I heard you aright): correctly, rightly

arse : ass, butt

askance (look askance at): disapprovingly

aspersions (cast aspersions on one's character): slander,
    doubt

assay : test

asunder (let no one put asunder): apart, separate

atomies : tiny beings, particles

attaint: dishonor, infect, corrupt, sully

attending : waiting

aught: any, anything; zero (as in nineteen-aught-six)

aumbry : cupboard or closet

avaunt: away

B

bade (farewell) : said goodbye

balderdash: jumble of words, nonsense —untrue

baldfaced (baldfaced lie): out-and-out falsehood

baleful : malevolent

bandy (bandy about): exchange, discuss, give-and-take

barefaced (barefaced lie): blatant

baseborn : illegitimate of birth —or of common parentage

bate: deduct, diminish, abate

bated (with bated breath): held, stopped

bawbling : insignificant

bawcock : fine man; from French beau coq

bawd : harlot, madame

beady-eyed: squinting, staring

bebother : wreak trouble upon

beck (at his beck and call): beckoning; summons

bedecked: adorned

bedfellows (Politics makes strange bedfellows): temporary
    allies, partners

bedight: equipped, adorned

bedizened: with tawdry adornment or decoration
    bedraggled: wet, muddy

bedridden: confined to bed

beetle : jutting, overhanging (as in beetle-browed)

beforehand: previously, before

befuddled: confused

begat: parented, gave birth to

begone!: go!, get away!

behest: personal request

beholden (I'm beholden to you): owing, in debt to

behoof: advantage, profit

behoove (it behooves you to ...): to profit, to be advantageous, proper, necessary

behove: to profit, to be of advantage

bejeezus (knock the living bejeezus out of): breath, fighting spirit

belabor (don't belabor the point): overemphasize

beleaguered: bothered

belike : perhaps, likely

bemused: amused, bewildered

benighted: ignorant; overtaken by darkness

bereft: stripped, abandoned, shorn, left without

beseem : befit, be appropriate for

beshrew : curse

besmirched (her reputation was besmirched): soiled, sullied

besom : broom of sticks and twigs

besotted: drunk

bespeak : order ahead of time

besprent: sprinkled over

besprinkle: sprinkle

bethink: think

betid/betided : happened

betide: happen

betimes: speedily, early; from time to time, now and then

betwixt: between

bewray: betray

bide (bide your time): wait; abide, have an abode

blatherskite: blusterer

blench : flinch

bodes : foretells

bollocks : nonsense; testicles

boon : favor, gift

boondocks (out in the boondocks): rural

boot : heavy shoe; to profit; (to boot) as well as, in addition

bounden (bounden duty): sworn

bower : area sheltered by hedges; inner room

brace : pair

brabble : squabble

brake : thicket

brazen : made of brass - or blatant ie: brazen hussy

brood : children

brook : face, endure, allow

bruit : clamor, ~~knock around~~ rumor

buck-basket : laundry basket

buck-washing : washing with lye

bugger : a curse; anal sex → *ie: to hell w/ it*

burthen: burden

buttery-bar : the Dutch door or half-door to the cellar or
place where beer and food provisions were stored.

buttery : pantry, store, wine cellar

button : clitoris

bygone (let bygones be bygones, bygone days): time past

byre : cow shed

cahoots (in cahoots with): collaboration, secret partnership

canker : disease

cap-a-pe : from head to toe, entirely

carbuncle : rounded gemstone, small ember

cataplasm : poultice

catch : catchy tune

catty-corner : opposite corner, diagonal

cattywampus : awkward; awry

cautel : wariness, deceit

cere : wrap, coat with wax

cerements : burial clothes

certes: certainly, in truth

chaffless : worthy

champing (I'm champing at the bit): eager, anxious to go

chary: suspicious

cheerio : goodbye, ta-ta

chid, chidden : chided, scolded

chine : deep ravine

cicatrice : scar from a wound

clave : stuck to, adhered

clepe : call, name

clomb: climbed

closet : bedroom

clotpoll, clodpoll, clodpole : stupid fellow

clouted : studded , *Hit*

cloven : split in two

cocked hat (toss that idea into a cocked hat): dismiss as a
possibility

cock-eyed: crazy, strange notion congeries: collection,
assemblage

codpiece : pouch at the crotch - *outer wear covering of male genitals*

coeval : born at the same time

coffer : strongbox, *chest, trunk*

cog : cheat

cogging : swindling, cheating

coil : fuss

colted : defrauded

commix : commingle

compass : accomplish *or include*

con : know, memorize

conceit : idea, suggestion, ~~false~~ *belief*

confusticate : baffle, confuse

contemn : treat with contempt

contumely: (heap contumely upon): invective, insults

cony/coney : rabbit, *slang for female genitals*

cony-catching : trickery

copse: grove

corse : corpse

cot : cottage, shelter

coted : skirted, went around

courtesies : curtsies

cozen : cheat, lie, deceive

cozenage : scam, swindle

crackerbarrel (crackerbarrel philosophy): homespun

craven : cowardly

crescent : waxing, growing

crestfallen: abashed, *disappointed, crushed*

crew : crowed

cropper (come a cropper): encounter an unexpected
obstacle, fail

crotchets : odd notions, crazy ideas

crowner : coroner

cuckold : husband with a cheating wife

cullion : testicle; bad person

cumbrous : awkward

currish : doglike

cudgel (cudgel your brains): think hard – *ur bash
in club*

cudgels (take up the cudgels): defend

custom : commonplace; transaction of a customer – *business, clientele*

cutpurse : thief

D

darnedest: best effort / dast (= darest): dares to) seperate entry

dastard : deceiving person

dastardly : evil

daubery : disguise

daunt : intimidate, discourage

dearth: lack

deck (deck the halls): decorate

deign: humble oneself to

depending : leaning

derring-do: bravado

descry: discover, reveal, espy ~~reassure~~

diaper : napkin

dingle : shady dale

dint (by dint of): blow, force, power, impress

dire (dire straits): dangerous, perilous

disedged : blunted

disgruntled: unsettled, unsatisfied

disport: play, gambol

divers : diverse

doddering (doddering old fool): wobbling, ~~confused~~

dolven : delved, dug out

doom : fate (not necessarily bad)

doornail (dead as a doornail): very dead

doublet : tight jacket, with or without sleeves

downtrodden: imposed upon, repressed

drab : whore

drabbing : whoring, sleeping with prostitutes

draff : dregs, cattle fodder

draught : draft; drawing; ship's safe water depth

drear: dreary

droves (they'll come in droves): crowds, herds

drumble : sluggish, slow

druthers (If I had my druthers ...I druther ...): wishes, alternatives

dulcet: sweet

dumfounded: astonished

durance : confinement, imprisonment

durn tootin': that's for sure

durst: dare

E

eaves : edge of a forest

e'en: even

e'er: ever

eftsoons : soon afterward

effrontery: gall, balls, chutzpah, *blatant discourtesy*

egad: I'm surprised, *exclamation of ~~alarm~~ (ye gods) suprise*

eke: also, increase, *~~squeege out of~~*

eld : old age

ell : tailors' measure of length, originally a cubit (elbow to middle finger)

embossed : exhausted

enchafed : heated, emotional

enow : enough

ensconced: safe, settled into, concealed

ere: before

erelong : soon

erewhile, erewhiles: until now

erst: once, formerly, in the past

erstwhile: once, former, previous – *~~meanwhile~~*

escoted : supported

espy : catch sight of

essay : attempt, try

even : evening

eventide

evitate : avoid, shun

exchequer : treasury

eyne : eyes

eyot : river island

F

fadge : succeed, ensue

faggot : bundle of sticks — kindling

fain: rather, pleased, willing, ~~compelled~~ prefer

fan : feign, to test → to pretend

fane : church, temple

fangled : gaudy, showy

fap : befuddled

fardels : burdens

farflung: widely scattered

fawn : grovel, cringe

fealty: fidelity, loyalty

feckless: ~~irresponsible~~, weak, ~~reckless~~ worthless

feign : pretend, act as if

fell: evil, cruel, sinister

fell swoop (in one fell swoop): all at once, all together

fender : fireplace frame

festooned: decorated

fettle (you're in fine fettle): demeanor, health

fey : heedless of the possibility of death oblivious otherworldy

fiddlesticks (possibly derived from violin bows): nonsense

fie!: for shame!

fief : lord's estate

finicky: picky

fixings : ingredients

flabbergasted: amazed, astonished

flagon : large mug

flibbertigibbet: scatterbrained

foible: weakness, minor flaw

foisted: forced another to accept, palmed off

folderol: unnecessary motions or procedures

foot : to pay, to pay for another

foreboding: sense of impending danger

forespeak : predict

foreswear : promise to refrain from, to break an oath perjure

forfend: prevent, forbid (heaven forbid)

forlorn: sad, lonely, abandoned

forsooth: in truth

forthwith: immediately, thereupon, from now on

fortnight : two weeks (fourteen-nights)

fosse: ditch, moat

fourflusher: bluffer?

fracas: fight

frampold : peevish

franklin : householder

fraught: (fraught with danger): full of; stink; freighted, carrying

fray (into the fray): battle, ruckus

freshet : stream or gushing water

froward: contrary, stubborn, habitually disobedient, ~~forward~~ *contrary*

fuddy-duddy: pompous person, *stick in the mud*

fullam : loaded dice

furlong : 660 feet

fust : mold, stink

G

gad (gad about): go out socially

gadzooks: I'm surprised, *exclamation of suprise*

gaged : engaged

gainsaid/gainsay (I won't be gainsaid): spoken against, denied, contradicted

gallimaufry : hodgepodge, jumble

gallivanting: roaming *< galoot - lts*

galore (bargains galore): plenty of

game : crippled

gan : began

garner : granary, *procured*

garth : enclosed yard or garden

gawds : baubles

geck : derision, contempt

gib : neutered male cat

gibbet : gallows

giglot : giddy girl

gimlet : boring tool in corkscrew shape

gin : snare, trap

ging : gang, crew

girt: gird, girded *~? define wrapped*

gloaming : twilight

glom (glom onto): grab

goggle : stare

goodman : "title" for those who have no title; ordinary male citizen

gramercy: thanks, astonishment

gravelled : confused, irritated

grist : grain prepared to be milled

grize : degree, step

grizzle : gray hair

guerdon : reward

gunwale/gunnel : top of ship's side

guying: ridiculing

gyves : shackles

H

habit : habitual clothing

hackneyed (hackneyed phrase): timeworn, *clichéd*

halt : lame

hap : happen

haply: by chance, by luck

happy : skilled

hark: listen

havior : behavior, demeanor

hayward : livestock keeper

hearken: be hopeful, listen, *pay attention*

heed : consideration

helter-skelter: scattered, random

hem and haw (stop hemming and hawing): hesitate, be undecided, ~~stall~~, *avoid giving direct answers*

hence: therefore; away, henceforth, from this time on

henceforward: from now on

henceforth: from now on

herefrom: from here

herein: within this

heretofore: until now

hew : chop, cut

heyday: height, acme

het (Don't get all het up): heated, angry

hie: go, hasten

highfalutin: snobbish, pretentious, pompous

hight : named, called

hilding : fellow of no worth

hindmost (The devil take the hindmost): last part, the
    remainder

hissy fit : temper tantrum

hither: here; closer to

hitherto: until now

hobnob : casual conversation, *keeping company with*

hoist with his own petard : killed or wounded by one's own
    weapon or strategem. Petard : a small explosive
    device to breach a wall

holden: held, ~~indebted to~~

hooey: nonsense

horn-mad : raving mad

hove (the ship hove into view): came, emerged

howbeit : although

hue and cry: outcry, *uproar (noisy)*

hurly : tumult, uproar

hummock : knoll, small hill

humor : attitude, temperament, *mood*

husbanded : handled, ~~took care of~~. *to have managed cautiously*

husbandry : taking care of one's possessions, saving

hustings: local election platforms

I

bad reputation (handwritten, left margin)

ilk: sort

ill-gotten (ill-gotten gains): loot, robbery money *acquired dishonestly* (handwritten)

ill-repute (house of ill-repute): whorehouse

immemorial (from time immemorial): unremembered, long ago

impending: about to happen

impone : wager, stake

inasmuch: since

incorporal : empty

ineffable: not tangible

inly : inwardly, with thorough knowledge

insofar as: since

insomuch: since

irregulous : lawless

it is: (a non-referent construction)

iwis : surely

J

jade : spiritless, weary; older horse out of condition

jerkin : jacket with no sleeves

jocund : light-hearted, *cheerful*

journal course : daily routine

journeymen : ~~apprentices~~, day workers — *adept at after ~~apprenticeship~~ before ~~master~~*

jump : just

having completed apprenticeship

K

kaboodle (the whole kit and kaboodle): all, everything

keen : sharp wailing, *mournful weeping*

ken (beyond our ken): ability to know, *knowledge*

kerb : curb

kerfuffle: commotion

kilter (out of kilter): adjustment, alignment

kindled : aroused

kindred (kindred spirits): close, related, *kindy disposed toward*

kine : cattle

kith (kith and kin): friends, neighbors

knickers: panties, underpants, *short pants worn by grown men fastened at the knee ie: knickerbockers*

L

lackaday : so sorry, *careless*

lam (on the lam): running away

laughingstock: object of ridicule

lave : bathe, wash

lay : a story song

league : three miles

leave : permission

leech : healer (leeches were once used to "clean the blood")

lest: for fear that

lickety-split: immediately

lief: gladly, willingly, *prefer to*

liege : person bound by loyalty to a lord, as the lord is liege
      to a duke or king *or title of lord ie: "yes, my liege"*

lissom : supple, lithe *lovely*

listeth (where it listeth): randomly chooses

livery : costumes of servants or soldiers

loll (loll around): lie down *→ uniforms (lazily)*

lorn: forlorn, lonely

lowlihead: lowly state

lubber : clumsy person

lurch (Don't leave me in the lurch): responsible for,
      abandoned, left unexpectedly

M

malapert : saucy, impudent

mantle : cape or cloak

march : border

mark : become aware of, notice, *take note of*

marry : indeed

maugre : in spite of

maw : jaws and mouth of predator

mayhap: perhaps

mead : honey-based alcoholic drink

☆mealy-mouthed: *cowardly* *worthy of contempt* *insincere*

meed : earned reward, gift

meet: precisely adapted, very proper, suitable, fitting

mere : pond or lake

meseems : it seems to me

methinks: I think

mew : to shut up, pen in

middling (fair to middling): mediocre, average

mind-boggling: astonishing

minge : vagina

mischance : accident

misgive : cause to doubt

misprised : mistaken, misunderstood

mode (à la mode) : with ice cream on top (the French
        phrase simply means, "in the current fashion")

moe : more

moiety : half

mongering (war mongering): encouraging

mollycoddle: pamper, ~~treat kindly~~ spoil, overindulge

moreover: besides, also

mosey (I'll just mosey along): go, stroll

moveables : furniture

mow : grimace

muster : assemble, collect together

N

nary (nary a one): not a single one

natheless: nevertheless, anyhow

naught: none, nothing

nay: no

needs (must needs): certainly, *have to*

ne'er: never

negro: person of African descent, black person

nether: under, behind, *below*

nethermost : deepest, lowest

nevertheless: regardless

newfangled: new

niggard : person who is reluctant to give or offer, *stinge*

niggardly : miserly, stintingly *stinginess*

nigger : mispronunciation of Negro (used as an insult)

nigh (well nigh impossible): near, nearly, almost here

noddle : head; noodle

noisome : obnoxious, offensive, stinking

nonce (for the nonce): time being

nonetheless: regardless

none the worse for wear: not noticeably worse off

nonpareil : without a peer

notwithstanding: regardless

nowise: in no way, absolutely not

nuncheon : light lunch

obeisance : bowing or kneeling, *curtsying*

ods bodkins: God's little dagger

o'er: over

offing (in the offing): near future, *being readied for the near future*

oft: often

oftentimes/ofttimes: often

onslaught: attack, *assault*

oodles: a lot of, many

ope: open

ornery: unnecessarily stubborn

ostler : stable master

othergates : otherwise

out-and-out : obvious, direct

overbear : overwhelm with greater number

overriding (overriding importance): great

P

painstaking: careful

pale : picket, stake

palfrey : lady's riding horse

palmary: outstanding

paltry: few, little

panderly : acceding to base emotions

panoply : full suit of armor

pardie : truly

parle : conversation, talk, oral treaty

passel: a lot, much

pate : head

pelf: booty, money, riches

pell-mell: in a rush, disorganized

pent-up: repressed

penury : poverty

peradventure: perhaps

perchance: perhaps, possibly

perdy : truly

perforce: by force of circumstances

perpend : ponder, reflect, consider

persnickety: particular

pheeze : comb, fleece, curry

phial: vial

physic : purge, remedy, *medicine*

picket : stake

pinchbeck: imitation, imitation gold

pish posh : no bother, don't worry, *or nonsense!*

plash : pool, puddle; splash

plumb (plumb tuckered out): completely

plumb (plumb the depths): explore

plurisy : excess, plethora

poppycock: nonsense

porringer : bowl for porridge

portend : foreshadow

portent : omen

pother: roiled

pottle : a two-quart mug

pray tell: tell

pregnant : convincing, *full (of)*

prenominate : aforenamed

pretty (pretty soon) : somewhat soon; not yet

primrose path : worldly pleasure

prithee : verily, *request, implore*

proem: prelude, preface

proffer: offer, tender

propound : express an idea for discussion

prosy : dull, commonplace

provender : food

p's and q's (mind your p's and q's): behave well puissance: power, strength

pudency : modesty

puissant : powerful

puling : whining, whimpering

punk : prostitute

purblind: blind, obtuse

purlieus : outskirts

purloin : steal

pursy : overweight, short-winded

puttock : a kite

Q

quaff : drink heartily

quail : be intimidated, shake (with fear)

qualms: fears

quarter : divide into four pieces; take up residence

quean : impudent woman, prostitute

queue: line

quiddit : equivocation, subtlety

quietus : death

quirk : ilk, peculiarity

quotidian : daily

R

rack (rack and ruin): ruin

raiment : clothing

rap : be emotional (present tense of rapt)

rapt : with full attention; focused

raring (raring to go): ready, eager

rat's tail (not worth a rat's tail. But that tale is nat worth a rake stele-rake handle. Chaucer, Wife of Bath's Tale): worthless\ ravening : hungrily eating

rayed : arrayed

read : advice

reck: worry, care, regard, concern, heed, understand

recountments : stories

recreant : cowardly, disloyal

rede : counsel, advise

redound: overflow, rebound, reflect, lead to unplanned consequences, accrue replete: complete

refts : berefts, takes away from

reins : kidneys

rent : rended, torn, tear

repair : go to

respite: pause, relief

ribands : ribbons

rick : haystack

rife (rife with): full of

rigmarole: complicated and probably unnecessary
      procedures, red tape

rill : small stream

riven: split *apart*

rollicking: having a good time

rood : cross

rough-hewn: roughly cut, *crudely made*

rough-shod: stepped on roughly,

rubious : deep red

rude : simple

runagate : renegade, runaway, as in cattle or horses let loose

ruth: compassion, sorrow, remorse

S

sable : black

sack : sherry

sallow : yellow skin

salver : metal tray

save : except for

scads: lots

scall : rapscallion, disreputable person

scathing: severe, terrible

score : twenty ⟨?⟩

scrivener : notary public *or scribe*

scuttlebutt: gossip

seigniory: authority, domain

sensible : visible to the senses, *aware of ones surrounding so*

sere : withered *conscious*

serf : peasant

shade : ghost, *spirit*

shag : have sex

shank : lower leg

shanks' ponies : walking

sharked up : gathered together shenanigans: tricks, doings

shend, shent: shame, revile, injure, ruin

shoon : shoes

shore : sheared, shorn, *trimmed*

shrift (give short shrift to): consideration

shriving : absolution *(after confession)*

simon pure: pure

sister-son : nephew

sith/sithens/sithence: since

skittish: nervous

skulduggery: secret plotting or actions, *underhanded dealings*

sleight (sleight-of-hand): trickery, magic

slew (a whole slew of): many

slipshod: poorly made or poorly done

slowcoach : slow or late person

slud: slid

smallclothes: underclothing

smit, smitten: struck, love-struck

smite: strike

smote: struck

so be it: let it be so

sojourn : temporary visit, *journey*

somedeal : somewhat

sooth: truth

soothfast : honest, truthful

spake: spoken

spang (right spang in the middle of): completely

sparge: spatter, spray

spinney : copse, small woods

spittoon : cuspidor; floor pot for spitting, provided for persons who chew tobacco)

splenetive : full of spleen, ill-tempered

springes : traps

sprited : haunted

squiffy : soft; inaccurate

stalwart: unwavering partisan, *strongly supporting*

staves : staffs; stanzas *as in weapon*

stead : position, place

stem : hold back

stithy : anvil, forge

stoup : tankard, bucket

strait : strict; constricted, *restrained*

strapping: robust

subtractors : detractors

succor : give aid

suffice (suffice it to say): is enough

sully: soil

sunder : separate, divide

surcease: discontinue

surety: certainty, assurance, guarantee

suspiration : breathing, sighing

swan (well, I swan): surprised

sward : lawn, meadow

swashbuckling: dangerous, adventurous

swinge : thrash, beat

swink : labor, toil

swoon : faint

T

tanlings : people tanned by the sun

taper : candle

tapster : bartender, tavern keeper

tarn : mountain lake

tarry : pause, wait, *loiter*

taxed : accused, *depleted (by or from)*

teen : grief

tetter : blister, eruption

thence: from there, there

thenceforward: from then on

thereby: from that, because of that

therefrom: from it

therein: in that

there is: (a nonreferent construction) *∼*

thereupon: after that event, *.. and then —*

therewith: with that, forthwith

therewithal: besides

thews : muscles

thither: (hither and thither): there

thraldom: slavery

thrall : slave

thralled : captive, slave, in bondage

thrawn : twisted; obstinate

thrice: three times

thriftless : useless, *careless*

throes (in the throes of): agonies

throng: crowd

throve : thrived

tidings : news

till : cultivate, plow

tilth : soil prepared for planting

tire : attire, headband

tithe : one-tenth, *regular payment of obligation*

to boot : as well (as), *on top of, ...*

todo: attention, *disruption or goings on > ado*

toils : trap, snare

toothsome : tasty — *very pretty*

tor : rocky hill

toss-pot : drunkard

tother : the other   *tother t'other*

traduced : humiliated

traffic : trade

traipse: walk, wander

trammel : net, trap

travail: work trice: instant

trenchers : wooden plates and trays *or large crust of bread used as a plate*

tristful : sad

troth (pledge my troth): become engaged

trove (treasure trove): discovery, cache

trow : understand, know, suppose

tryst: secret meeting

tunic : long flowing garment, usually sleeveless

Turkey cushions : Turkish-style pillows with tassels

turnkey : jailor

turves : turf; slabs of grass and earth

tussock : grass clump ← *twzddle*

twain : two

twixt: between

two stones : testicles

U

umbel : flowers on a single stem, as parsley

umbrage (take umbrage at): be offended by

unbeknownst: unknown

uncouth: unmannered

unhouseled : not sanctified for death

unmarked : unnoticed

unpaved : unstoned, castrated

unperturbed: calm

unquiet : anxious, concerned

unrecked : not considered, abandoned

unrequited: not loved in return, *unreciprocated*

unsated : not satisfied

unscathed: untouched, unharmed, not wounded

unto: to , *until*

unwieldy: awkward

unwonted: rare, unusual, undesirable, *unwelcomed*

urchin : imp, brat, unruly child, *street children. orphans*

usward : toward us

vailed : lowered, downcast

vale : valley of a river

van : vanguard, *most forward*

varlet : servant, knave

vassal : servant

vaunted: reputed

vendible : saleable; corruptible

ventages : airholes

verily : truly, confidently

vesture : apparel, clothing

vicissitudes: ups and downs, hazards

victuals/vittles : food, provisions

videlicet : that is to say

vie : contest with, rival

vigil : watchfulness, *or kept watch*

vouchsafe: grant, allow, *guarantee*

waif : homeless child

wain : wagon

wan: sickly, pale, feeble, languid

wanker : masturbator, *annoying person*

ware : aware

wassail : pledge or salutation signified by drinking alcohol *or celebration*

wax : grow stronger, increase

waylay : intercept, *accost*

wayworn : unkempt from traveling

weal : happiness, prosperity

weeds : clothes worn for mourning (widow's weeds)

ween: imagine, hope

welkin : the sky, upper air

wellaway : alas

well-nigh (well-nigh impossible): almost, nearly

wend: travel, roam, proceed

weskit : waistcoat

whatsoever: whatever

whelm : submerge, overwhelm, cover

whenas: when, since

whence: wherever, from where, by reason of, wherefore

whereat : for which reason

whereby: from which, because of which

wherefore: why, therefore, for what reason; reason (whys and wherefores)

wherein: in that

whereof: of which, of whom, with

whereon: on which, in which, that with which

wherewith: with which, in which, with what. by means of which

wherewithal: resources, usually money, ability (to)

whet (whet your appetite): sharpen

whilom : formerly, once

whit (not one whit): bit, jot, iota

whither: where

whizbang : startling; marvelous

whomso: whomever, whoever

whomsoever: whomever

whopping: huge, outrageous

whosesoever: of whomever, anyone (who)

widdershins: wrong, contrary, counter-clockwise

wight: fellow, creature, stalwart, spirit

wile : deceit, trickery

willy-nilly: at random, carelessly

wis: know

wist : known

wit (to wit): namely, specifically, that is to say

withal: besides, nevertheless

wizened: wrinkled

woebegone: sorrowful, depressed

wold : moor

wont (as was his wont): habit, inclination, liable , desire

wood : insane, wild

worst : defeat

wot: know, learn

wrack: (wrack and ruin): destruction; driven clouds

wraith : apparition, ghost

wreak (wreak havoc): bring upon writ: wrote

wreathe : engulf, surround

wrest : seize

writhen : twisted

wroth : angry

Y

yammer : wail, whine; complain

yare : nimble, quick

yclept: named, titled

ye: you

yede : to go

yoicks : expression of surprise

yoke : oxen harness; complete control

yon (hither and yon): over there

yonder (wild blue yonder): there

yonside : on the farther side

yore (days of yore): long ago

Z

zenith : highest point

zip it: shut up

zounds: I'm surprised

Iffy Words

aforesaid: previously stated

aghast: unpleasantly surprised, horrified, disgusted

avail (to no avail): uselessly

ballyhoo: advertising, noisy promoting

befall: happen

betrothed: engaged to be married

bevy: small group of birds

bosh: nonsense

by and large: more or less, usually

covey: small group of birds

crop up: occur unexpectedly

deemed: considered

dole (on the dole): welfare

dole out: distribute

far-fetched: unrealistic

fine (in fine): specifically

forfeit: give up without contesting

forsake: give up

full-fledged: complete

furthermore: and besides

gaggle: group of geese

gingerly: cautiously

hale: healthy

hankering: yearning

hoopla: media hype, enthusiastic publicity

hubbub: stir

ill at ease: uncomfortable

list: incline, lean, tilt

miffed: insulted, feeling snubbed

pallor: paleness

peeve (pet peeve): annoyance

ruthless: merciless

save: but, except

sought: looked for

steadfast: unshakable

taken aback: surprised

underhanded: not openly, illegal

Made in the USA
Charleston, SC
07 February 2014